...LET'S HAVE COFFEE

The Tao of

Ian Holloway

Collected by **Alex Murphy**

This is a **Toilet Book**

Toilet Books™

Publishers: Steve Faragher, Richard Jones

Design: Joe Burt

ISBN 0-9544177-9-8

The first moral right of the author has been asserted

Front cover picture supplied by Empics

First published in Great Britain in 2004 by Toilet Books, an imprint of
faragher//jones ltd, The Studio, Little Theatre Cinema, Bath BA1 1SF

Printed by Short Run Press in Exeter

this book is dedicated to

Jo, Tom and Will

" To put it in gentleman's terms, if you've been out for a night and you're looking for a young lady and you pull one, you've done what you set out to do. We didn't look our best but we've pulled. Some weeks the lady is good-looking and some weeks they're not. Our performance today would have been not the best-looking bird, but at least we got her in the taxi. She may not have been the best-looking lady we ended up taking home, but it was still very pleasant and very nice, so thanks very much and *let's have coffee.* **"**

Ian Holloway describes QPR's performance against Chesterfield in September 2003

2

Contents

Ian Holloway's career statistics

Born: Kingswood, Bristol—12th March 1963

Ian Holloway played 603 games
in a 20-year professional playing career

As a player

Club	Year	Fee	Appearances	Goals
Bristol Rovers	1981-85	Apprentice	111	14
Wimbledon	1985-86	£35,000	19	2
Brentford	1985-86	Loan	13	2
Brentford	1986-1987	£25,000	16	0
Torquay United	1987	Loan	5	0
Brentford	1987	Recall	1	0
Bristol Rovers	1987-1991	£10,000	179	26
QPR	1991-1996	£230,000	147	4
Bristol Rovers	1996-2000	Free	112	11

As a manager

Club	Year	Games	Won	Lost	Drawn
Bristol Rovers	1996-2001	190	83	53	54
QPR	2001-Nov 2004	247	90	87	70

6

From the West has risen a footballing sage whose words of truth have transcended the mundane realm of sport.

Ian Holloway, the Buddha of Bristol, is a lone voice of wisdom in a mad world of insanity and lies. His earthy homilies have delighted journalists in quest of a quote, and he has never failed to deliver. But his utterings amount to far, far more than the dribblings of some cut-price Rent-a-Gob.

Students of Holloway's teachings can discern a clear, coherent philosophy, which encompasses all areas of human endeavour and embraces the mind, the body and the spirit.

There are uncanny parallels between Holloway's message and one of the greatest texts in the history of world thought: the *Te Ching*, Tao Buddhism's sacred text.

To follow the path of Ollie enlightenment, come with us on a journey through the Tao of Ian Holloway...

異

Being Different from from Ordinary Men

Sayings

" I got them from my father who had more sayings
than you can hang your hat on. **"**

Size

" Now I'm a little fella as it happens, but when
I was really small I was nothing. "

People

" My dad taught me life is about people, it ain't about where you come from or who you are. You should be able to stand in a room and talk to anybody, learn from everybody and love them for who they are.**"**

Trials

" Bristol City came in first and all they talked about was how brilliant I was gonna be and when you're 16 we'll give you this, and when you're 17 we'll give you that, and when you're 21 you'll play for us and you'll never have to buy another pair of boots Mr Holloway. In fact here is his size right now. And out they go. And in come Bristol Rovers and all the fella says is 'you did alright today, you were quite fair. Now if you want to be a good player son, you've got to want it more than the next fella and all we are guaranteeing you is you got to work hard, you got to be dedicated and it's down to you and it's down to you how good you can be. We know you might have a chance, but it's down to you son.

Now, who do you think I chose? I chose the people who told me the truth. I wasn't a big head, I knew what it was all about—you gotta work hard—mould yourself into something. **"**

Ollie reveals why he chose Bristol Rovers as a nine-year-old boy

Maybes

" If is a big word. If I had long hair I could be a rock star. **"**

Height

" [Georges Santos] is a big lad. He can clean out your guttering without standing on a ladder. "

Labels

" I call [Jerome Thomas] Ronseal. He does exactly what it says on the tin. He's an out and out winger. "

Goal Celebration

" [Richard Langley] over-elaborated with his celebration.
He looked like a chicken stick. "

Mentors

" I was lucky enough to work with Gerry Francis for nearly 10 years at two different clubs. Until I met him I thought I knew a lot about football. After I met him I knew nothing. **"**

Appearances

" If you can keep your noses in front at the end, that's what counts. It's been said that I have a bit of a Roman nose and I am keeping it ahead at the moment. Hopefully it's all about the length of your hooter because I might be in front at the end of the season as well. **"**

Holloway looks forward to life as QPR boss

A Caveat against Violence

Team Talk

" I want you to bad rash them. **"**

Meditation

" I'm trying to learn how to relax. I'm now going to take my brain out and stick it in an ice bucket. "

Flat Batteries

❝ Once we had got the equaliser I wanted to put jump leads on my players because I thought we had an excellent chance of nicking a win.**❞**

Holloway electrifies his QPR team after a 1-1 draw at the City Ground

Referees

" The refereeing was very one-sided but I will take my medicine. I got incensed and said one or two swear words I'm not allowed to say. It's ironic you can get sworn at and intimidated all day and if you show emotion you're in trouble. I'm pleading guilty and I have apologised to the referee. But football is about passion and the day I don't care is the day I give up. **"**

March 2002, Holloway is keen to discuss the referee's performance after a 1-1 draw at Cardiff

Linesmen

" It was lucky that the linesman wasn't stood in front of me as I would have poked him with a stick to make sure he was awake. "

Strength

" We've got to be solid and horrible to break down.
I don't want to be southern softies. **"**

Strikers

" You can say that strikers are very much like postmen: they have to get in and out as quick as they can before the dog starts to have a go. **"**

Ruthlessness

" It's no good counting your chickens. Even if we're 2-0 up with five minutes to go on Saturday don't think we've already done it, we've got to kill it off, hold people down and strangle the life out of them. "

Sufficiency and Quietness

Money

" You have to ask about a bar of soap at this club. I even had to pay for our pre-match meal on my own credit card on Saturday. **"**

With QPR facing administration Holloway tightens the purse strings

Hair

" Gareth Ainsworth is the most physical winger I've seen. He calls himself the wolf man because of his sideburns but I don't pick fault with hairdos if players perform. "

Tactics

" When you play with wingers you look a bit like a taxi with both doors open, anyone can get in or out. **"**

Predictions

" I am a football manager. I can't see into the future. Last year I thought I was going to Cornwall on my holidays but I ended up going to Lyme Regis. **"**

Internationals

" Richard Langley looked like he was still in Trinidad and Tobago playing for Jamaica. He's got to realise what it's all about. It's not just him, it's all of them, but I'll start with the big ones and work my way down, because that ain't good enough. "

Holloway incandescent after QPR lose an FA Cup replay to Vauxhall Motors on penalties

Pianos

“ The trouble with us is that we've had too many players sitting at the piano, not moving it. **”**

Holloway highlights Bristol Rovers' shortcomings even after beating Bristol City 2-0 at the Memorial Stadium

Success

" Every dog has its day—and today is woof day!
Today I just want to bark. "

April 2004, QPR win at Sheffield Wednesday to earn promotion

Motivation

" One of their members of staff has been rude as f*** about us, so it's about us coming out on top. It's not about pretty football, it's about winning football. We've got to go out today. Let's get on our f***ing toes. Let's get in here. All my life I've been on a crusade because you can be a winner without being rude. Get f***ing focussed. Get in nice and tight. Feel that f***ing strength. **"**

Ollie rallies his QPR players before a 2-1 home win against Brighton

Being and Not Being

People

❝ I'm a people person and I can't wait to work with these people. **❞**

Man Management

" We're on the crest of a slump but you won't get me criticising the players. I feel like I've been mugged. "

April 2000, Bristol Rovers lose against Preston

Wisdom

" A week is a long time in football. **"**

Nature

" You never count your chickens before they hatch. I used to keep parakeets and I never counted every egg thinking I would get all eight birds. You just hoped they came out of the nest box looking all right. I'm like a swan at the moment. I look fine on top of the water but under the water my little legs are going mad. "

Sportsmanship

" I hope we don't get a situation where teams refuse to put the ball out of play, for the obvious reason that some injuries can be serious or even life-threatening and immediate treatment is vital. This is not just about Bristol Rovers losing two points. This is an issue for all levels of football to consider, from the Premiership down to the Dog and Duck versus the Gasworks. "

Nerves

" It was tense and I was dying for the toilet. As soon as Kevin scored, I went. **"**

Injuries

" He's been out for a year and Richard Langley is still six months away from being Richard Langley. **"**

Belonging

" You can't suddenly tell someone that they have got to drive 20 miles to support their team—it just doesn't work. I'm very proud of this place. This is our tribe, we are strong together and this is where we live. I like this cave we are in and I want to keep living in it. That's as blunt as it has got to be. "

Holloway in full flow after stories emerge of a plan to shift QPR from Shepherd's Bush to Heathrow

Strikers

" I always say that scoring goals is like driving a car. When the striker is going for goal, he's pushing down that accelerator, so the rest of the team has to come down off that clutch. If the clutch and the accelerator are down at the same time, then you are going to have an accident. **"**

Referees

❝ I have never seen such a stonewall penalty kick in all my life. Even my wife in St Albans could see that it was a penalty. ❞

Caravans

" Everyone calls him a gypsy but I can assure you he doesn't live in a caravan. He has a house with foundations. "

Ollie on QPR defender Gino Padula

Change

" When the water stands still in the pond, it starts to stink. **"**

Danger of Overweening Success

Desire

❝ It takes a brave man when the crowd is against you and you're 1-0 down to stand there and want it. ❞

Losing

" I can't stand losing. I don't know what it is. Whether it's a personal thing I don't know. It just seems so much more than a game. When I'm not in control and I want something and I want it now and I can't have it, then it don't work. I normally go mad. **"**

Patience

" I don't want to be patient—I want promotion. **"**

Chocolate

" If the club was a chocolate bar, it would have licked itself. **"**

On QPR in the Premiership

Ice

" The club isn't on solid ground. It's like I'm on a block of ice. I don't know whether I'm going to go through it, or slide off. **"**

On the QPR he inherited

Pies

" [QPR] is the people's club and everybody can have a piece of that pie. A pie that's already smelling beautifully. "

Health

" As a club we are out of hospital now and we are looking forward to the convalescence and being fighting fit for the future. "

Wages

❝ I don't think he would get his left toe out of bed for the wages we would pay him. **❞**

Ollie rules out a swoop for Sergei Rebrov

Money

66 There was absolutely no plan whatsoever, except to stay in business. The finances were that dire, we've had days and weeks where that was it, we nearly stopped. None of us has ever shown it, we've just got on with it. It's the *Men in Black* thing, sometimes you're better off not knowing. It hasn't been easy but it's been thoroughly enjoyable. 99

Ollie reflects on difficult early days at QPR

Aliens

" Did anybody see the *Men in Black*? Well I've got a little black suit on and so has David. We've got a little black bow tie and we've got some glasses and every now and again we are going to have to go PHTTTT with this little thing to lose your memory. Because, what you don't realise is that over the last year, we have been so close to the brink of someone wanting to steal the Galaxy, that we were in big, big trouble. **"**

Ollie reassures worried QPR fans at Hammersmith Town Hall in 2001

The Value Set on Life

Mortality

66 My day didn't start very well. The Holloway household had to have our dog put down unfortunately, but that's life. I've just said to the lads: 'You're born and you die on a date. You've got to work on the dash in the middle'. 99

Selling Players

" When [QPR] seemed to be dying, we were a carcass and the vultures came and fed off our bones. "

Concerts

❝ It's all very well having a great pianist playing but it's no good if you haven't got anyone to get the piano on the stage in the first place, otherwise the pianist would be standing there with no bloody piano to play. **❞**

Medicine

" The doctor grafted a bit of Danny [Shittu]'s hamstring onto his knee, but that won't be a problem for him. He's got more hamstring than the rest of the squad put together. **"**

Play-off Defeat

" It's one of my proudest days in football, but I've caught the bouquet again. I'm always the bridesmaid. "

Epitaph

66 That's what they're going to put on my headstone: 'Here lies Ollie: he tried'. 99

Leading from Behind

Supporters

" Most of our fans get behind us and are fantastic. But those who don't should shut the hell up or they can come round to my house and I will fight them. "

Holloway blasts QPR boo-boys

Support

" It's all about togetherness from top to bottom and at the top is our fans. You don't get anywhere in life without spirit and the fans are joining together to show that. **"**

Knowing your Place

" We want to get the ball behind the opposition—not just smashed, but in behind their full-back and centre-half. I don't pay Danny Shittu to pass the ball. I don't pay him to be pretty, I pay him to defend and be in the right place because he's a big monster. Him and Clarke Carlisle have got to sort their lives out and defend for us. **"**

Defending

" We need a big, ugly defender. If we had one of them we'd have dealt with County's first goal by taking out the ball, the player and the first three rows of seats in the stands. "

Holloway gets technical after a worrying defeat at Notts County

Rewards

“ If the players think they can get away with it they are very much mistaken. Under my regime they need to show pride and passion in every game. The days of picking up your pay packets at QPR are gone. **”**

April 2002, and Holloway opens negotiations over QPR players' contracts

Pre-Season Training

" I took them orienteering on Monday—and two of them got lost. We had to go out in a van to get them. I can't tell you who they are because they are a little embarrassed. **"**

QPR's team-building summer trip to Scotland has a hitch

Perceptions

" We're no longer the flitty farty QPR. **"**

Hospitality

❝ What we've all got to do is pick him up, slap him around and make him feel welcome. **❞**

Ollie's remedy for a foreign signing's homesickness

Sailing

" We've picked the ship up off the bottom of the ocean, plugged a few leaks and we're floating on the top. Now we want to turn around and sail off into the sunset. **"**

Fat Ladies

"The fat lady might be picking the mic up but I can't hear her singing yet.**"**

Hindsight

" It's easy to say after the event 'Holloway should have done this, Holloway should have done that' but that's after the event and funnily enough that's when Holloway realises it as well. "